It's CHRISTMAS!

ALL ABOUT
SANTA

KRISTEN RAJCZAK NELSON

PowerKiDS press™

NEW YORK

Published in 2020 by The Rosen Publishing Group, Inc.
29 East 21st Street, New York, NY 10010

First Edition

Editor: Kristen Nelson
Book Design: Reann Nye

Photo Credits: Cover, p. 5 Kiselev Andrey Valerevich/Shutterstock.com; p. 7 Zvonimir Atletic/Shutterstock.com; p. 9 Hulton Archive/Getty Images; pp. 11, 15 Victorian Traditions/Shutterstock.com; p. 12 Everett Historical/Shutterstock.com; p. 13 wongstock/Shutterstock.com; p. 17 Bettmann/Getty Images; p. 19 Library of Congress/Corbis Historical/Getty Images; p. 21 JStone/Shutterstock.com; p. 22 LightField Studios/Shutterstock.com.

Library of Congress Cataloging-in-Publication Data

Names: Rajczak Nelson, Kristen, author.
Title: All about Santa / Kristen Rajczak Nelson.
Description: New York : PowerKids Press [2020] | Series: It's Christmas! | Includes index.
Identifiers: LCCN 2018046599| ISBN 9781725300842 (pbk.) | ISBN 9781725300866
  (library bound) | ISBN 9781725300859 (6 pack)
Subjects: LCSH: Santa Claus-Juvenile literature. | Christmas-Juvenile
  literature.
Classification: LCC GT4992 .N45 2020 | DDC 394.2663-dc23
LC record available at https://lccn.loc.gov/2018046599

CPSIA Compliance Information: Batch #CSPK19. For Further Information contact Rosen Publishing, New York, New York at 1-800-237-9932.

CONTENTS

SANTA, TODAY

Santa Claus is the number one **symbol** of Christmas in the United States today. He's shown in movies and is part of songs throughout the season. But the stories of Santa told today have been a long time in the making. They started with a Greek **bishop** and mixed with ideas from **cultures** around the world!

4

5

SAINT NICK

Saint Nicholas of Myra lived during the third and fourth **centuries**. He was a Christian bishop in present-day Turkey. During his life, Saint Nicholas often helped the poor. In one story, he gave a man three bags of gold so the man's daughters could marry and wouldn't have to work.

7

After Saint Nicholas died, people started **celebrating** his life on December 6. Across Europe, children were given gifts on this day. However, after about 1500, people in many places stopped celebrating the day as much. In the Netherlands, though, the gift bringer they called Sinterklaas continued to leave children presents the night before Saint Nicholas's day.

ACROSS THE OCEAN

Europeans settling in North America brought their holiday celebrations. Dutch settlers brought their **tradition** of the gift-giving Sinterklaas. German settlers continued their **custom** of the gift-bringer Christkindle visiting children on Christmas Eve. Over time, the many traditions began to mix. "Sinterklaas" became Santa Claus to those living in the young United States.

ART ADDS TO THE STORY

By the early 1800s, the story of Santa as it's told today was taking shape. Some ideas came from a tale by famous writer Washington Irving. In the book *Knickerbocker's History of New York,* he wrote of Saint Nicholas flying in a wagon and giving presents to good children.

WASHINGTON IRVING

13

A poem written in the 1820s didn't use the name Santa Claus, but it added a lot to his modern story. In "A Visit from Saint Nicholas," Clement C. Moore describes Santa's good nature, white beard, sleigh, and reindeer. He also has Santa deliver gifts and travel up and down the chimney!

15

Cartoonist Thomas Nast began drawing Santa for magazines in the 1860s. His drawings showed an elf-sized man who looked like a grandfather. Over the many years he drew Santa, Nast also added a red suit and workshop at the North Pole to Santa's story. His **illustrations** shaped what Americans thought Santa looked like.

AD MAN

Santa Claus's look today can likely be traced to **advertisements** for the drink Coca-Cola! Illustrator Haddon Sundblom began drawing the ads in the 1930s. He showed Santa as a full-size man with a white beard and a red suit, reading letters from children, delivering toys, and drinking the soda.

COMING TO TOWN

Today, Christmas movies and books about Santa Claus add to the traditions that began with Saint Nicholas more than 1,500 years ago. Most are partly set at Santa's home, the North Pole. Some suggest that Santa has been living for hundreds of years. Others include his wife, Mrs. Claus!

Whether he's called Sinterklaas, Pere Noel, Kris Kringle, or Father Christmas, Santa is a symbol of the magic and good cheer of Christmastime. He reminds us of the fun of giving gifts to those we love, as well as those in need. Believing in Santa makes the season of Christmas even better!

GLOSSARY

advertisement: Something that is shown to the public to help sell a product.

bishop: One who leads the members of a church in a certain area.

celebrate: To do something special for a day or event.

century: A period of 100 years.

culture: The beliefs and ways of life of a certain group of people.

custom: An action or way of behaving that is common among the people in a certain group or place.

illustration: A picture or drawing in a magazine or book.

symbol: Something that stands for something else.

tradition: A way of thinking or doing something within a group of people.

INDEX

WEBSITES

Due to the changing nature of Internet links, PowerKids Press has developed an online list of websites related to the subject of this book. This site is updated regularly. Please use this link to access the list: www.powerkidslinks.com/IC/santa